The Minin

Copyri

Dedicated to Mara, Sadie, and Camille,
the three girls I love the most in the world.

A special thanks to Matt Duckworth for helping get the
thoughts out of my head and onto paper,
Joni Wilson for editing, and
Kristie from 2Faced Design for the cover art.

Contents

Chapter One

Why Write a Book on Money for Teenagers?

When it comes to building wealth, the most powerful force you have on your side is time. As the days and years pass, the opportunity to build wealth by leveraging time slowly dwindles. The idea for this book came from the realization that often times kids start working their first job at sixteen, likely just a minimum wage, or near-minimum wage, job, but they haven't been taught how to accumulate wealth. I wasn't.

In high school, I had some basic accounting, and I learned how to balance a checkbook. We did some stock market games to learn a little about investing, but no class I took ever laid out a plan for success in a capitalist society. No class I took talked about the "Rule of 72," or compounding return on investment over time, or tax advantaged investment accounts.

But all of those things I just mentioned are critical to understand in a free market capitalist society. They are critical to understand from the moment that you earn your first dollar. It doesn't matter how wealthy or poor your parents are, it doesn't matter what background you have, all teenagers in the United States, after reading this book, can set themselves on a path to build a staggering amount of tax-free cash. With just a little bit of knowledge about how money works, and the discipline to follow through, you can be in control of your financial destiny.

I'm embarrassed to admit that I have not taken advantage of the time I've had to accumulate wealth. Worse than that, I realize that as the years have passed and other financial obligations of adulthood have grown, setting aside extra money becomes more and more elusive. I have to acknowledge some hard facts about my own bad money habits—bad habits that stopped me from building wealth. I have to reflect on wasted opportunities and bad decisions. Finally, I have to draw some tough conclusions about the consequences of not saving and investing.

But it doesn't have to be that way for you. After reading this book, you will have both knowledge and youth on your side. You will have an action plan on how to start accumulating wealth now. And the possibilities before you will be endless. But let's talk about where bad money habits start.

Why?

Because I've sucked at money. I mean, if blowing a paycheck were a sport, I'd be Muhammad Ali—the greatest of all time. As a kid, I didn't know any better, but it starts a pattern.

When I got my first job as a paperboy at 12 years old, I immediately took the money from my first paycheck down to the Ben Franklin, a few blocks from my house, and bought a bottle of Coke and tons of baseball cards. On the way home, I stopped at Mickey's for a Chicago-style hot dog with all the fixings and some fries. By the end of the week, all the money I'd made was gone. Back then, it wasn't much, but today—if I'd just invested part of that somehow—I'd have enough to buy a small island in the Bahamas. I was too young to know it, but that was my first big missed opportunity.

If that's not painful enough to look back on, I'm sad to say it didn't stop there. When I started my first real job in high school (bagging groceries), after work, the arcade ate quarter after quarter. And then there were movies (I thought everyone went to see *Raiders of the Lost Ark* 20 times!), gas for the car, games for Atari, and the occasional burger, french fries, and Coke. It all added up.

Paycheck after paycheck was burning a hole in my pocket. I wasn't saving or investing anything, but at least I had to stop when there was no money left. Credit cards would later solve that problem. After college, I moved to California, bought a new car, new furniture, new wardrobe, and lots of new grown-up toys. I started getting my hair cut at a trendy salon with a French name, moved into an apartment in the "hip" part of town with a pool table and a pop-a-shot.

You know what's truly sad? It took me a LONG time to learn from my mistakes. As I got older, people warned me to start saving. I can remember my dad getting near retirement age and shaking his finger in my face at the dinner table on Thanksgiving, saying "You'd better invest your money for retirement, or you're gonna end up working until you die!" but I ignored him. The years rushed by, and then, with my net worth still bobbing near zero, my wife and I got pregnant with our first baby.

As I sat in the hospital in Chicago—never again. I must change. I must be a good example. I can't let them suffer the same mistakes I made. I started saving like crazy in my company retirement plan. And that lasted for a few years, but the economy changed, and I was not prepared. I was unemployed for a while—longer than I ever imagined. The mortgage, the bills, it consumed far more than the unemployment check.

I began working a part-time job for minimum wage at the local big box store, but unlike my teenage years, the meager paychecks didn't help much with all the bills. As the Great Recession continued, I eventually cashed out the retirement money, penalties and all, so I could keep paying the mortgage. It still wasn't enough. In the end, I lost it all, the house, the savings, and Best Buy even stopped by to get their TV back. I was sick to my stomach.

Listen. I honestly wasted all my opportunities to build wealth and have the choices, the options, to retire rich, so that I don't have to work until I die, so that I can spend my time with my family. Now, knowing how easy it is to get there if you start early and seeing the principles in this book work for so many people, I'm ashamed of my past actions. But you don't have to have my same regrets.

So how does a guy who lost everything know so much about creating wealth? That's a valid question, and I'm glad you asked. Learn from your mistakes. As you grow up, you'll likely hear that over and over from your parents, teachers, and coaches. It's what I've had to do myself. Learn from my mistakes. So the rest of this book is about what I've learned.

In life, there are no do-overs. I can't go back and make things better for me. But for every teenager out there, hope springs eternal. If this book can make an impact on just one kid (besides my three beautiful daughters), I've accomplished more than I could possibly imagine. I've created this book is to help you understand what an amazing opportunity you have right now. Time is on your side, and every day that goes by, you lose a little bit of your opportunity. Don't make that mistake. Don't make my mistake. In the following chapters, I will lay out for you exactly what you need to do to build wealth.

I warn you, it won't come quickly, and it won't be easy all the time. In fact, there will be moments in your life when you question whether or not what I've told you is true. You'll want to go back to your old ways and you'll have pressure from friends to spend, spend, spend!

When in doubt, just remember, the tools you're using are the same principles that thousands of people have used time after time to become the wealthiest people in the world. You're in good company.

My great hope is that you'll realize just how incredible an impact a little bit of savings and planning will have on your life. If you can just avoid my mistakes and save smart, you can really, truly become a minimum-wage millionaire.

Chapter Two

Things You Never Knew You Should Know

This may be the most important time of your life. You're in school. You're figuring out whom you are and what you want to do with your life. You've got lots of options and time to get good at something while still under your parent's care. You don't have to worry about bills, a mortgage, your career path, a spouse, kids, or taking care of your aging parents (all the things your parents worry about).

Now, this is not one of those books that's going to tell you to be more responsible, stop having fun, and concentrate everything on the future. I believe your youth should be spent having fun, experiencing new things, and learning about how life really works. In fact, on average, you'll only have this level of independence and freedom from worldly worry for just 10 percent of your life. You better squeeze the most out of this time as you can.

The point of this book is to show you that your youth can also be an incredible time to begin creating wealth, because it's so easy. You're living with your parents and they pay for all your food, clothes, and most of your other expenses. Any money you earn from work is usually a bonus. Whether you spend half of it or all of it really doesn't have a big impact on your lifestyle or happiness. All this puts you in the ultimate power position—freedom to easily invest money for the long, long-term.

To illustrate what I mean, you've got to understand what's about to happen to you as you leave the care of your parents and go out on your own. Here are just a few facts:

- The Department of Education states that only 68 percent of high school graduates enrolled in college the following fall. If you aren't going to college, don't panic. This book is still for you.
- In 2013, the average annual price at a public four-year

institution for tuition, fees, room and board, was $16,789. Most students pay for some or all of their tuition by borrowing money.

- According to the National Association of Colleges and Employers in its 2013 survey, the average starting salary for a college graduate is $45,327. If you have an engineering/science or computer programming degree, you'll get paid a little more. Everyone else (except for business majors) tend to get paid less than the average.
- At $45,327, that means you'll be taking home about $2,800 per month after payroll deductions.
- With your remaining $2,800 you'll have to pay for rent, food, gas, utilities, TV, internet, cell phone and your student loan payment. Maybe there is a car payment and insurance. On average, you'll spend about $2,000 on all this. That leaves you with $800 left. Great! But wait—
- You still have to buy clothes, get your oil changed regularly, go to the movies, take a little vacation, and eventually you'll have to buy a new car. Oh, and those are your expenses if there are no emergencies (and I promise you there will be) and you aren't helping to support a significant other or child. After it's all said and done, most young people are lucky to have $100 left over to save or invest each month.
- To illustrate the difficulty in saving after high school, the average 18–24 year old carries almost $3,000 in credit card debt (source: debt.org).

Realize that once you're out on your own, saving money gets really hard. There's always one more thing that needs to be paid for, and when you're young and not earning much, it's tough to cover all your expenses. It can be even tougher without a college degree.

That's how a lot of people who get married and have kids end up being 40 or 50 years old before they can really start to save and invest for their own future, and by then it can be too late. So, right now you've got a golden opportunity. Quite literally—a once-in-a-lifetime opportunity. The concept of starting small and building wealth now or even imagining a time when you are beyond your best income earning years is such a far-off thing. It doesn't even seem real, and this makes it hard to prepare for it, especially when you've got a cool new gadget or a new pair of shoes you want to buy. The day is coming whether you plan for it or not though. It's already set in stone.

I hope I can help you see that there's a real need for you do a little prep.

More Reasons Why Investing Now Is Crucial
- A college education is still the surest way to earn more over your lifetime. The only problem is that tuition is skyrocketing, so even if you make more money, you'll likely still have a mountain of debt to carry once you're done with school. And it can take a decade or longer to pay off student loans. Also, imagine what a debt burden means for your happiness. Will you be able to pursue a career you enjoy, even if it pays less?
- Some degrees don't carry extra earning potential. While a college degree can open some doors to jobs that are out of reach for non-degree holders, those jobs can feel like sweat shops. Everyone who needs a job is applying, the company pays as little as it can to fill the spot, and the boss will crack the whip to make sure you're working your fingers to the bone, because there's another poor kid clawing at the doors to take your spot. If you're an art major, planning for your college degree to magically whisk you away to the land of fun, high-paying jobs, then put in your mouthpiece. Your dreams are about to get kicked in the teeth. Also, remember that if you borrowed to get your degree, you'll have Uncle Sam asking for a check every month.
- Life has surprises. Just ask any adult you trust. When you get out into the real world, surprises will spring up that always threaten to snatch money from your wallet. It's called Murphy's Law—anything that can go wrong will go wrong. Sometimes they're just minor expenses, such as a speeding ticket, and other times they're major life-

shaping events, such as getting pregnant, a major medical issue, or a natural disaster. Whatever it is, life has a way of sending financial challenges your way on a not-so-irregular schedule. Often times, it's those money-sucking surprises that keep you from saving throughout life.

My advice? Just use your brain. You're smart enough to know that life isn't going to go as planned, so preparation is in order. If you're onboard with that, let's move to the next chapter.

Chapter Three

Why Most People Won't Follow the Plan

"Genius is one percent inspiration and ninety-nine percent perspiration."

—Thomas A. Edison

When I was a kid, my grandfather encouraged me to get a business degree and pursue a career as a stockbroker. He had been a stockbroker for Merrill Lynch and said it was a great career move. But, I was interested in computers. Computers were new, they were fascinating, and they were the future. I spent hours programming and learning about how they worked. Looking back at that conversation, I should have realized that he was giving me this advice while we were golfing at a private country club at which he was a member.

I understood completely why my grandfather wanted me to pursue the career he chose. It would no doubt change my life and open up many doors. The fact was, however, that I just wanted to hang out with my friends, play baseball, and program on my computer. I wasn't worried about the future. I was having fun where I was.

Although it's hard to tell for sure, it probably would have been wiser to get that business degree, looking back on it. That's human nature though. If it's not our idea, we don't want to do it. That's exactly why this chapter exists. Even if this is the most life-changing information you'll ever read, you probably won't use it. Studies show that only 10 percent of people who buy a book actually read the whole thing. It's just the way we're wired.

Even if you read the book, you've still got to follow the plan. Here are some of the major reasons most people won't:

Too Impatient
Being impatient is part of being an American. We hate to wait for what we want. If it takes longer than 30 seconds to get our food at McDonalds, we're steaming. If it takes longer than 10 seconds to

find what we're looking for on Google, we're updating our Facebook status to let the world know. Inevitably, you'll be tempted to either not start this program or—if you do start—to touch the money in your account early.

Here are just a few examples of ways people let impatience get the best of them:

- You see the new amazing dream car, and you can't say no to the salesman. You buy it.
- Your girlfriend/boyfriend keeps mentioning how much he/she wants to go on vacation to Mexico and doesn't have any money. You end up footing the bill.
- You get married, and your spouse desperately wants a new house in which to raise your future kids. Instead of renting a house until you have more savings and higher income, you cave in and buy the house.

The other thing you need to realize is that patience is partially genetic. Yes. Some people are actually designed to be able to delay gratification longer than others are. This is one reason why generational poverty exists. Some people just don't have it in them to say no to the new car, a fresh lotto ticket or another pair of designer blue jeans.

For those of you who are worried that you're doomed to be poor, the good news is that investing for your future is a habit that can be acquired, so don't let genetics be an excuse. You just have to be aware that you are wired a certain way so you can manage yourself.

In addition, your youth puts you at a disadvantage because you don't have as many experiences to draw from that remind you that you're doing something stupid. Most teenagers can't look back and say "Remember that time when I screwed up my whole life by buying lots of things on my credit card I couldn't afford? That sucked." Most older people have those memories. That's why they're always trying to tell you what to do. They've already screwed it up once, and they don't want you to suffer through it as they did.

Often times, those stories aren't enough to convince you to follow their advice. That's normal. You end up learning the hard way, and you slowly gain more respect for those stories. That's life. Hopefully you can just take my word for it though.

Your Parents' Bad Money Habits Rub Off on You
Most people don't realize just how much their parents influence their thinking until much later in life. The fact is, your parents have a huge impact on how you think of money. If your parents work for someone else, it's likely they think in terms of security and predictability. They like receiving a paycheck on a specific day for a specific amount, and they like knowing that they can take the weekend off and not have to worry about other people's problems. Employees tend to focus on their ability to trade their time for money. They may build expertise in something and earn a lot of money, but at the end of the day, they get paid by the hour.

If that sounds like your parents, stop and ask yourself how you feel about the term "security." Does it feel good? Is that what you are looking for in a future career?

If so, your parents' thinking has probably rubbed off on you.

Here are some other beliefs that you might pick up:

- Being wealthy is evil.
- You shouldn't want money because it makes you greedy.
- Spend your money and have fun. You don't know if tomorrow is your last day on Earth, so enjoy yourself.
- There's no need to control your spending, because things usually take care of themselves.

Some of the beliefs, that people with influence in your life have, will be good and beneficial. Other times, their advice will be terrible because they're repeating something they picked up from their parents, a friend, or the media, and they never questioned it. You are responsible for what you believe, so understand the impact that the people around you are having on you. Then you'll be in a much better position to live the life you really want.

Don't Understand the Time Value of Money

Most people don't look at a dollar and think about how it's actually worth more than a dollar if saved and invested wisely. This is the fundamental rule of building wealth, so if you don't understand this principle you'll never build wealth. You may get lucky, you could win the lottery or hit the mega jackpot at a casino, but it will be just that—luck. Your whole focus in life—if you want to become wealthy and possibly create generational wealth—is to take your dollars and put them in investments that give you back more than a dollar. That's the whole trick.

In fact, deciding to understand and use the Time Value of Money to your advantage can be one of the most important decisions you ever make in your life. It can literally change everything. You can go from being a regular Joe with an average job to a real "player" in the game of life, if you just pay attention to how you use your dollars.

If you don't decide to use the Time Value of Money, however, you're likely doomed to mediocrity. Even if you become a brain surgeon, you'll never get really rich.

Fall in Love

Some young romantics spend their money on their significant other, because they think that is what love is about. I feel for them, because I've been in their shoes. I was living in California, and my girlfriend was originally from Phoenix. I surprised her with tickets to see the Chicago Bulls play the Phoenix Suns. I had a limo and airline tickets plus tickets to the game. It was a fun night, but it really set me back financially. The relationship didn't last, but the financial sting of that one date lasted a lifetime. If you want to build wealth, avoid the emotional and unaffordable expenses.

True love is about doing what's best for the long-term benefit of your significant other, and the most loving thing you can do is to be responsible with your money so that, as you get more mature, you can take care of each other, spend quality time with family, enjoy life, and not be forced to continue working. This is true love. Buying your girlfriend a new diamond necklace or a Jamaica cruise is fun and may get you in her good graces, but you must realize you're stealing from your spouses' future "need" to fund a present "want."

That's not love, my friend.

It's hard to resist the desire to impress. We're genetically programmed to impress the opposite sex, so you must realize you're fighting your DNA. We sometimes see what our neighbors bought and decide we want it to, regardless of our family budget. It's called "keeping up with the Joneses." That's why you'll almost definitely have a moment of weakness after you've saved a significant amount of money where you want to pull out some cash for a gift to your significant other. Don't do it. When that time comes, remember what I told you. One day, far down the road, you'll be happy you stuck to your plan.

Finally, before I step off my soapbox, I need to make one more point. Relationships are hard on your money, because when you really like someone, it's hard to say no. Saying no is one of the most important skills you'll ever learn as you grow up, because it's really tough.

You'll get asked to do certain things that compromise your future, your reputation, your time, and your money. One day, someone will offer you a job you should say no to. You'll be approached about an investment you should pass up. You'll be pressured to date someone you know you shouldn't date. All of these moments are important, because we never get to see how our lives would be better if we'd said no. It's tough to learn from those kinds of experiences, but they're just as important as any other lesson.

Won't Finish the Book
About a decade ago, there was a study done that asked people to list all the books they'd bought in the last year and how much they'd actually read. The study showed that, on average, most people would only read about 10 percent of a book—usually the first chapter. I doubt this book is any different.

One of the main obstacles to having a plan for your financial future, if you're like most people, is finishing this book. The good news is that if you've made it to this page, you've got momentum. Do whatever works for you, but don't let your momentum slow down. When your momentum slows down, it gets harder to finish what you started.

Focus on keeping your momentum up, and you'll be able to say you were one of the 10 percent who actually finished what they started. In life, you'll be surprised how much you'll accomplish if you just live by that one rule.

Now that you know what will trip you up, let's take a look at the basics of how to become a minimum-wage millionaire.

Chapter Four

How the Rich Get Richer

Have you ever wondered why some people are so wealthy, even though they're not any smarter or harder working than most other people are? Seems unfair, right?

How did they get there? Do they have better connections? Did their parents give them money? Did they take out a huge loan and gamble on starting a business? Is it from illegal or shady activity?

While these myths may be true for some wealthy people, for the most part, getting wealthy is pretty simple. It comes from having the right "strategy."

What is this secret strategy you ask?

Diversified Investing + Small Deposits of Money + Time = Wealth

I'm calling it the "six-year stretch" because if you can make those small deposits of money over the first six years with your part time job, you'll be in great financial shape. You will have found a way to earn money while you sleep. It's this little kernel of knowledge that forms the strategy that the wealthy use to get richer and richer. Let me explain.

You see, most people work for money. Wealthy people have their money work for them.

Most people go to a job and trade their time for money. They go to a job, sit at a desk, take orders from a boss, and then on Friday go home for the weekend with a paycheck. No more worries until Monday. No investment is required. The owner of the business they work for is fine with this too. He uses the worker to grow his business, and he's willing to pay for that service in cash. He takes the financial risk, but he gets to keep all the reward.

Rich people don't think like employees. Rich people don't trade time for money. They invest money to get a return without having to do any of the work. They find a good investment, put their cash in, and, if they've chosen well, they get more money back than what they've invested. They keep doing this over and over, until they wind up with A LOT of money.

The Employee Strategy requires lots of time and effort, and you don't get to decide the rules. The Investor Strategy requires little time and effort and often you get to make the rules up. Sounds pretty cool, right?

So, if getting rich is so simple and obvious, why doesn't everybody do it?

Your beliefs in money are passed down from generation to generation or inherited from your friends or culture. If your parents were poor, chances are you'll be poor too. If your parents were rich, chances are you'll be rich too. People tend to stick to the beliefs and strategies they were raised with.

So, if your dad worked construction all his life for someone else, chances are you'll end up working for someone else your whole life too. If your mom owned a furniture store, chances are you'll grow up to own a business too. We tend to do what we're familiar with, without even thinking about it.

But take a minute and go to the Forbes Richest List. I doesn't matter what year you look at. Just go look. You'll see one thing in common with all of them—there are no employees! Not even a world-renowned heart-surgeon or a top-paid, super lawyer! All of the richest people in the world invest to make their money work for them, because they know their earnings are capped, if they just trade time for money.

So, which group do you want to be in?

Two Choices
I'd like to demonstrate the importance of patience when investing, because the results will take what seems like an eternity to manifest themselves. Patience is a virtue, especially when investing money. Let's say I'm the richest man in the world, now if you read Chapter

One you know I'm most definitely not, but let's imagine this together. Ah, I'm doing a good job of imagining. Now, I have to hire two people to do a job for me.

In both of the jobs, for the next 30 days you have to drive around delivering copies of my book to all the bookstores, libraries, and schools. I did say that I was imagining this, right? The only difference between the two jobs is the pay, and you have two choices. With choice #1, I will pay you a flat $10,000 per day, every day, for the next 30 days. With choice #2, I will pay you one penny on day one and double your pay every day up to day 30. Which would you choose?

My imaginary friend, Gary, took choice #1, the $10,000 per day and my other imaginary friend, Melissa, took choice #2. Let's see what happens. The first week they both do a great job and my book is delivered all over the place. I'm extremely happy. Gary picks up his paycheck, and it's for $70,000. He worked all seven days this week at $10,000 per day. He is really excited.

After cashing his paycheck, he goes out and buys a new Mercedes and pays cash. He's contacted a real estate agent about possibly moving into a bigger house. Melissa, on the other hand, didn't do so well. She picked up her paycheck for $1.27. She got one penny on day one, two pennies on day two, four pennies on day three, eight pennies on day four, sixteen pennies on day five, thirty-two cents on day six, and sixty-four cents on day seven. A whopping $1.27. She was wondering how she was going to pay for groceries and rent!

The next week flew by, and I was happy to see that my book was making it to more and more bookstores. I paid my two employees again. Gary got his check for $70,000, and Melissa got her slightly larger check of $162.56 (1.28 + 2.56 + 5.12 + 10.24 + 20.48 + 40.96 + 81.92). Gary was able to buy the house he really wanted with a big back yard and a pool. Melissa was not sure if she could afford to keep the electricity on in her apartment.

The third week of the month was another great week. I could see my book featured in almost every bookstore in town. My two employees were both doing a great job. I paid Gary his $70,000 for a job well done, and Melissa got a larger sum of $20,807.68 (163.84 + 327.68 + 655.36 + 1,310.72 + 2,621.44 + 5,242.88 + 10,485.76), but still much less than Gary. She could at least afford to pay off her car loan and still have rent money.

So, going into the last nine days of the 30-day employment, I had already paid my two super excellent employees: Gary had earned $210,000, and Melissa had earned a total of $20,971.51. Quite a large difference in how much each was paid, but I could see where Melissa's patience and delayed gratification was starting to pay dividends.

The last nine days were a blur. Books delivered everywhere. My two employees hit all the high schools, libraries, and big box stores. I couldn't wait to hand out the final paychecks. Gary's paycheck was pretty easy to figure out, nine days, $10,000 per day, so that's $90,000.

I handed Gary his final check and thanked him for a job well done. He earned a grand total of $300,000! Not bad for one month's work. Now I had to figure out Melissa's final paycheck. I noticed that her checks were starting to get pretty big. Let's see, 20,971.52 + 41,943.04 + 83,886.08 + 167,772.16 + 335,544.32 + 671,088.64 + 1,342,177.28 + 2,684,354.56 + 5,368,709.12 = **$10,716,446.72**.

Melissa's check was for ten million, seven hundred sixteen thousand, four hundred forty-six dollars, and seventy-two cents! Wow!

So at the end of the month Gary was paid $300,000, and Melissa was paid $10,737,418.23. Who was the big winner here? Which person looked like they had the better deal after the first week? After the first three weeks?

Gary represents an employee collecting a paycheck. Even if it's a really, really good paycheck of $70,000 per week, it stays the same, or if you're lucky it goes up a little bit each year. Your paycheck, if you work the same number of hours each week will be the same amount every single time. And at minimum, or near-minimum, wage, your paycheck might seem like Melissa's after week two; but invest and have patience.

The Rule of 72!
You've been learning math in school since the first grade, maybe even kindergarten. Every year it gets a little more complicated, but happily, what you're about to learn next is at about the fourth grade level, so no worries, right?

Here's an important fact to remember. **Money makes more money.** For example, when you deposit $100 into a bank account that pays 1 percent interest, at the end of the year you will have $101. The extra one dollar you earned is the interest paid for your deposit, and it is yours to keep, forever and ever. Now, if you left the $101 in the same bank for another year, at the end of the year you'd have $102.01. Why the extra penny? It's because the dollar you earned as interest last year is now making money for you! That dollar earned its own penny. Congratulations!

So then, what's this "Rule of 72" all about?

It's a simple way to figure out how many years it will take to make your $100 turn into $200 without you adding any more money of your own.

Let's say you have a choice among three different banks to deposit your $100.

1. Tightwad Savings and Loan—pays 3 percent interest
2. Fair and Balanced Credit Union—pays 6 percent interest
3. Generous Bank and Trust—pays 9 percent interest

It's pretty clear that the Generous Bank and Trust will give you the most bang for your buck by paying a high 9 percent interest, also called your rate of return. If you made the $100 deposit and the rate of return never changed, how long would it take to double your money? That's where the Rule of 72 comes in handy.

1. Tightwad Savings and Loan

$$72/3 = 24 \text{ Years}$$

2. Fair and Balanced Credit Union

$$72/6 = 12 \text{ Years}$$

3. Generous Bank and Trust

$$72/9 = 8 \text{ Years}$$

Do you want your $100 to turn into $200 in 24 years? 12 years? or 8 years?

I think we'd all agree that doubling our money in 8 years is better than 12 or 24 years.

So, How Does This Help You Get Rich?

The Rule of 72 is a simple way for you to understand the massive power of saving while you're young. You want every $100 you save to double and double and double as many times as it can. Unfortunately, the banks listed above are mythical; no banks are paying a high rate of return for savings and, historically, banks offer a lower rate of return than other investments. The stock market over the past 100 years has a rate of return right around 9 percent, and over your lifetime—if nothing crazy happens—you can probably expect about the same returns.

So, let's work this out real quick. If you're 16 now, and you save $100, let's figure out how much that will be worth when you turn 64.

Well, number one, if your hundred dollars grows at 9 percent, you know your money will double in 8 years.

Number two, you know that you have 48 years for the money to grow.

So how many times will your money double in 48 years? Six times—

And what's $100 worth, when you double it six times? Watch this:

1. $100 x 2 = $200
2. $200 x 2 = $400

3. $400 x 2 = $800
4. $800 x 2 = $1,600
5. $1,600 x 2 = $3,200
6. $3,200 x 2 = $6,400

$6,400!! WOW!!
What if you just saved $1,000 from a summer job one year?
That's $64,000!! Not too shabby!

Compounding Interest
"Compound interest is the eighth wonder of the world. He who understands it, earns it . . . he who doesn't . . . pays it."

—Albert Einstein

In the example above, your $100 investment grew to $6,400 over 48 years when your return was 9 percent a year. That should be setting off some light bulbs in your brain right now. Every dollar you invest today could be worth $64 to your future self. The $5 lunch at the hamburger restaurant today is taking $320 from your future self.

This is why it's so critical for you to start saving while you're young. Over long periods of time, your money compounds—snowballing from just a few crumpled up ones to a massive truckload of Benjamin Franklins! If you're patient enough and smart enough to invest your money now, while you still don't have any major expenses, you're going to be MILES ahead of your friends later in life. A lot of the worries that most people have, as they get older, won't even cross your mind, because you'll be sitting on fat stacks of cash.

Qualified Savings Plans
The last piece of this puzzle is the place you're going to save your money. A few years ago, the government passed a law that created the perfect place to save your money, and I'll give you a hint, it's not a savings account at a bank. To put it in financial speak, it's called a Qualified Savings Plan (QSP), and the type of QSP you want to use has special powers.

The idea behind a QSP is that you store your money in a safe place, and it grows and grows. In a perfect world, when you get ready to start taking some of the money out, you don't want to be taxed on it. Surprisingly, our elected officials actually created that perfect world for you! They created a special QSP that lets you deposit money, let it grow, and then withdraw it without paying tax on the gains.

Taxes eat up huge amounts of people's hard-earned money each year. Yes, taxes are necessary for our government to run, but most people end up overpaying on taxes, because they don't know how to legally use every opportunity they have to avoid them. Wealthy people, on the other hand, take every advantage they can get to keep the money they've earned in their own pocket.

That's where the Qualified Savings Plan comes in.

Have you ever heard of Fort Knox? It's an army base in Kentucky. Since 1937, the Treasury Department has stored all the gold owned by the United States at that one location. Imagine how much security they must have to protect all that gold. Now imagine that your own wealth-building account is in a location similar to Fort Knox and protected with big-armed security guards with machine guns and tanks guarding it from all sides. The government has declared that your wealth-building account is a national treasure and anyone who tries to get into it without authorization will be shot dead on sight. This doesn't scare you, however. You own that account! In fact, each two weeks you take some of the money from your paycheck and send it to your secure wealth-building account.

Over the years, your balance in your account grows to $10,000, and then $100,000, and then $500,000, and eventually $1,000,000, and people start to take notice. Senators, representatives, businesspeople, and local officials look at it with envy—they want in—but they know that if they try so much as to even touch your account, they'll be executed by the guards without so much as a blink.

Then one day, after many years of letting your money grow in your special account, you decide it's time to cash some of it out. You walk down to the bank and, as you go to open the door, the guard stops you. There's a tense moment as he stares you down, but then he recognizes your face. He waves you through, and you go grab your cash in the vault. On the way out, as all the politicians, the IRS, and other envious onlookers watch you push your huge wheelbarrow of cash out of the bank lobby, the armed guards stand by your side to make sure that you get to keep what's yours.

In a sense, this is what a Qualified Savings Plan is. It's a special tax-safe account that allows you to save money and grow it tax-free. Now over the years, the government has created several different types of plans for individuals and employees of some businesses, because they really do want you to have options to become wealthy. I'm not going to discuss all types of plans, because it's mostly a jumble of letters and numbers like IRA, 401k, and 457, to name a few. The one we want to focus on like a laser beam is called the Roth IRA.

All you need to remember right now is that, unlike a traditional bank account, once your money is inside that Roth IRA, as long as you follow some simple rules, no matter how big your account gets, the government can't take a dime of your money!

Chapter Five

How to Save Smart

One night as I walked into the living room, my three daughters were watching a reality TV show called *Toddlers & Tiaras.* You may have heard of it. Competition-crazed moms push their tiny young daughters to the limit to win beauty pageants, and sometimes money. I thought it was all ridiculous, but while I was working on the computer, I couldn't help but watch as the drama unfolded.

On this particular episode, a young girl won the title of grand supreme something or other and the top prize was $1,000 cash. The money was paid in crisp one hundred dollar bills attached to what looked like a fan so the little girl could display her winnings to the whole audience. "Wow!" I thought to myself. "Not a bad day's pay for a five year old!" Did the little girl get to keep the money? Probably not. I'm guessing that her mother used the winnings to buy more glitzy dresses, spray tans, and other necessary pageant items.

Honestly, that made me kind of sad. Not because the little girl was being dragged from competition to competition by her mother. It was because I knew just how much a $1,000 payday could REALLY be worth to that little girl, and her mother likely spent that money without even asking. You see, if you or I saved $1,000 and were smart enough to invest it and refuse to touch it, that money would likely be worth upward of $250,000 when that little girl gets into her sixties. Her mother had no idea how costly her decision was, or how it would affect her daughter's life in the distant future.

Sadly, people make mistakes like this all the time, because they don't understand the principles taught in this book. My goal is to help you see that just a little savings while you're young will go a long, long way. I guarantee you. It's worth the sacrifice.

Let's use a more relevant example that probably hits a little closer to home. The summer I turned 16, I got a job working at a local grocery store as a one of those cart wranglers and grocery bagger. I was getting paid about $5.75 an hour then and working 20–25 hours a week usually, so in a typical week I'd make about $130 after taxes. It wasn't much, but it bought me as many root beer floats from Dog n Suds as I could stand and some money for movies and the arcade.

That first year I made about $5,000 dollars. If the Roth IRA had been invented back then, and I'd opened an account and invested $4,000, and blew only $1,000 on myself—today, that $4,000 investment would be worth about $43,000, and projecting the investment into my sixties, it would be worth around $200,000. And all I had to do was just skip a few root beer floats and trips to the arcade!

It's really important that you understand that saving like this only works for what's called "earned income" because smart savers put money in special government approved savings accounts—and these accounts can only accept money that's considered "earned" income.

For our purposes, earned income is simply money you get from working a regular job. You work at the grocery store or the golf course, you get paid for a few hours of delivering newspapers, and all of these are earned income. If you bought a lottery ticket and won $50,000, that wouldn't fit the IRS definition of earned income, because you really didn't earn it. The government says you got lucky. Anything that doesn't look or smell like a regular job is often not earned income, so beware of that. For more information, you can always search the topic online, go to the IRS website, or contact a tax professional, if you have questions about earnings from your work.

Once you've "earned" income, you can put it into the qualified savings plan we discussed in the last chapter. You put money in and it gets to grow tax-free, you pay zero taxes while your money's in the magic Roth IRA account.

This is different from putting money in a regular bank account. When you invest inside a regular bank account, your earnings get taxed. As your money grows, your gains are taxed. A tax here, a tax there, all those taxes can really add up to some serious money! Over a lifetime, a few tax payments can literally be worth MILLIONS!

That's why it's important to save the right way—by putting earned income into a Roth IRA.

Investing smart is not just about what you do. It's also about what you don't do. Once you've started saving earned income and putting it in the right type of savings bucket, you'll be overwhelmed with all the investment options you come across. Most people go from one investment to another based on how they feel, a hot tip they heard from a friend, or some story they heard on the news. This is what smart investors try to avoid.

You see, most professional investors spend decades learning how to get better returns in the stock market and most of them fail over the long-term. It's really, really hard. There's a lot of research to suggest that for most of the people who get better returns than the general stock market in a given year, it's almost all because of luck.

Smart investors try to ignore the emotions of greed and fear. They don't try to "get in" when they think the market is at its lowest point and try to "get out" when it looks like it's at the high. Because often times even the smartest investor is just wrong. We will discuss wise investing for a teenager further in the next chapter.

Chapter Six

Investing Wisely

Now that you've got a little bit of an overview of how to build wealth, it's time to talk about some of the details that will allow you to get started. We've talked about the important role that rate of return and time play in creating wealth, but how should a teenager invest wisely?

Diversification

Let's say you're at a carnival. Walking around you stumble on the booths where they have the games of chance set up. You see the ring toss, where you try to throw a little plastic ring on a Coke bottle from a few feet away. There's the squirt gun derby where you spray a stream of water onto a bull's eye to make your horse run faster to win the race. And next, you see a wall of balloons and a man holding darts. Let's use the balloon-and-dart carnival game to illustrate diversification.

As you step up to the game, you notice that there are hundreds of small balloons attached to a wall, and you're handed a sharp dart to throw at the balloons in hopes that you'll break one. Imagine that each of those balloons represents a different business. On one of the balloons is written IBM, another has Apple written on it, and Facebook, and Twitter, and on and on.

You carefully aim your dart at the wall of balloons. When you throw your dart, whatever balloon it hits, means that company is going out of business. Bankrupt. Investors lose everything. You throw the dart and it pops a balloon called Enron. Bye bye. Enron. It's gone. If you had all your money in Enron, it's gone too. Now there's still a whole wall full of balloons, and they are all perfectly fine. Not a scratch on them, but the poor Enron balloon is popped for good.

How would you feel if all of your money was invested in the balloon that popped—a company that went bankrupt?

But how would you feel if a little bit of your money was invested in every single balloon? Sure, one popped and that's bad, but your investment in all the other balloons is perfectly fine. Overall, you take a small loss instead of losing it all.

Diversification is investing in lots of the balloons and not just one or a few.

Indexing
A stock index is the measure of the value of a group of stocks that make up the index. Different indexes are derived from different formulas. But to keep it simple, an indexed fund is based on the idea of diversification, which means that you spread your risk over a bunch of different investments—a "basket" if you will. Even if a few of the investments go down, on average, the value of the basket tends to go up.

I like to describe an index as a diverse garden and investing in an index is like investing in the garden. One of the most popular indexes is the Standard and Poor's 500, and it represents 500 of the biggest companies in the United States. It's often called the S&P 500.

Let's imagine that each company in the S&P 500 index is a plant in our garden. A section of our garden is dedicated to trees and shrubs, another section to flowers; another is made up of fruits and vegetables, and so on. It is a diverse garden that provides us with everything. Many, but not all, of the plants provide us with some dividends in the form of food, wood, or medicine.

Sometimes, however, a plant withers and dies and needs to be replaced. The gardeners come in and take out the old dead plant and replace it with another vibrant growing plant while always maintaining a total of 500 plants. Thinking of an index as a diverse garden is one way to visualize what the investment looks like. For your reference, a complete list of companies in the S&P 500 index is provided at the end of this book. I think you will recognize many of the companies. You might even get a job working for one of those companies. Then you'd be a worker and an owner. Investing in an index means you become a small owner of each of the companies in the index.

Index investing is a smart and simple strategy. As a teenager or young adult, it creates the diversification you need, and it can provide excellent growth over a long period of time. In fact, the strategy we're about to show you has averaged a nearly 10 percent return over the last century. It's solid.

Smart investors like to "set it and forget it." They have a long "time horizon" that allows them to sleep well at night knowing that it doesn't matter what the stock market is doing today. As long as they've got the right strategy, they know they're going to make money.

The stock market could rocket up 1,000 points, and smart investors don't get excited. It could go down 1,000 points, and they wouldn't flinch. They know that, in the long run, it'll probably go up about 10 percent a year, and they're happy with that. The only thing that matters to the smart investor is that businesses continue to make money and grow in the long term. If that happens, their investment will grow.

Which Investments to Use
Once you've made up your mind that you're going to invest by indexing, you need to know the "How To" of finding the right investment choice. Your first step is to identify which investment you should buy.

This can get really complicated. In fact, there are people who get paid a lot of money just to figure out which investments their clients should make. As I said earlier, as people get older, their financial life gets complicated. Luckily, for you, your financial life is still simple, and this book has a narrow focus. It's likely that you fit into the following categories: young, debt free, limited income, and patient enough to build your wealth over a long time.

Because this is a book, and we can't give every reader individually tailored investment advice, I've created a simple plan that will work well for almost any young person who's got a long time before they need to tap into their wealth and can stomach seeing some wild swings in the stock market. It's likely that over the next 40+ years, you will see at least two or three steep declines in the value of your investments. These steep declines are sometimes called a stock market "crash" or a "panic." It's normal. Something in the world happens, and everyone decides at the same time that it's time to sell. Never feel that you have to do what everyone else is doing.

Keep investing, every paycheck. Keep building your wealth, every paycheck. But where are you going to invest your money? Earlier we talked about the S&P 500, a group of 500 large companies. But how can you invest in 500 different companies at the same time? It's a problem that's already been solved.

Years ago, people wanted to invest in a diversified group of stocks, but alone nobody had enough money, so they pooled their money. The pooling of money to buy a group of stocks is called a "mutual fund." Today there are quite literally thousands of mutual funds. You should focus on one type of mutual fund called an S&P 500 index fund. Why? An index fund owns all 500 stocks, and it's designed to mirror an index. If S&P decides to remove XYZ Corp. and add ABC Corp., the mutual fund will do the exact same thing. So the S&P 500 index fund is diversified, and it doesn't cost much to buy.

Mutual Fund Fees
Read this section and then read it again. All mutual funds have fees. The fees are paid by you and all the others who've invested in the fund. How much you have to pay can make all the difference in the world for your future wealth. Remember, we estimated that every $1 in your account today is $64 in your future account. So—every $1 you pay in fees today is $64 less dollars in your future account.

You can see how this adds up over time. Here's a simple illustration. Buying any mutual fund other than an indexed fund will cost you on average about 1-2 percent in fees. By comparison, an indexed mutual fund will cost you about 0.25 percent. You may be saying, meh, who cares. But think about it. If both funds average 9 percent per year for 40 years, and you have to pay 2 percent in fees, you're only netting 7 percent.

$5,000 invested with an annual 9 percent average return for

40 years = $152,046.99.

$5,000 invested with an annual 7 percent average return for
40 years = $74,872.39.

That 2% difference may seem small but over time, it will add up.
Over 40 years it amounts to over half of your total possible return.
All other investment trades have a commission. Often times, even
though the commission is only $5 to $10, on a small biweekly
investment, it is huge. For your situation, an S&P 500 indexed
mutual fund with no upfront fees and a very low annual fee likely
works the best.

Dollar Cost Averaging
Dollar cost averaging is the tool that you're going to be using to get
good returns on your investing for a long time to come, so let's get
acquainted with it.

When you dollar cost average an investment, it basically means that
instead of throwing all your money into the market at one time, you
invest small chunks of cash over a long period of time. Think back to
our garden example and think of your money as water for the
garden. Making one big purchase is like opening a fire hose on the
garden and then never watering it again. Not the best way to keep it
healthy. Instead, water the garden a little each time and the plants
will love you.

So, here's an example. Every month, you buy some shares of your
S&P 500 index mutual fund. The price one month is $10, the next
month it's $12, and then maybe the next month it's $8. Over time the
cost "averages" out and, because of some cool laws of mathematics,
your returns are almost always higher over the long run.

This is because you are buying when the market is high and low—
and when you buy low, your dollars actually purchase more shares
than when you buy high (duh, right?). All of this works together to
make your account grow. The chart below shows what dollar cost
averaging looks like. The monthly investment is a steady $400 but
the share price changes from month to month. As the share price
changes, the number of shares purchased each month also changes.

The share price starts at $10 and throughout the year it goes up and down but ends the year at $10 again. You might think that because the share price started the year and ended the year at $10, you break even. However, because the share price went up and down, you came out ahead.

	Monthly Investment	Share Price	Shares Purchased
Month 1	$400	$10.00	40
Month 2	$400	$12.50	32
Month 3	$400	$16.00	25
Month 4	$400	$10.00	40
Month 5	$400	$8.00	50
Month 6	$400	$5.00	80
Month 7	$400	$8.00	50
Month 8	$400	$12.50	32
Month 9	$400	$10.00	40
Month 10	$400	$8.00	50
Month 11	$400	$8.00	50
Month 12	$400	$10.00	40
Totals	$4,800	$10.00	529
Value of Investment		$5,290.00	

So, what this means for you is that you'll be taking money from each paycheck you get and putting it into your Roth IRA account. If you get paid once a month, have your employer set it up so that part of your check (for example, 25 percent) gets deposited directly into your account once a month. If you get paid once every two weeks, do the same but just have the money deposited every two weeks when you receive your paycheck, if your employer will do it. This way, your savings are automatic.

When you don't have to touch and feel the money before you save or invest it, it becomes much easier to save. You don't want to be tempted to spend your savings. Direct deposits into your savings account ensure you avoid that temptation.

Setting up Your Account

First, let your parents know what you plan to do. If you're under 18, the brokerage will require a parent signature to open an account. We suggest you set up your Roth IRA with a major online brokerage firm, such as Schwab or Fidelity. These online brokerages have low fees and good service so that if you have any questions, they'll get answered promptly, and your money goes as far as it can.

When you sign up for your Roth IRA, you'll need your social security number, driver's license, your employer's address, and beneficiary information (in case you die, they've got to find who to give your money to). If you go online to Schwab or Fidelity, you'll find an application for your Roth IRA. You or your parents can call them so they can walk you through the process if you have trouble.

After the account is set up, you'll need to put money in your account. You can have money automatically drafted from your bank account each month or, if your employer will do it, you can have them send the money to your Roth IRA straight out of your paycheck before you get it.

How Your Brain Can Kill Your Investments
"When others are fearful, be greedy and when others are greedy, be fearful."

—Warren Buffet

The most basic advice that we can give you is to avoid doing stupid things. If you just follow that one little principle, you're almost guaranteed to have a good life. Unfortunately, human beings are hard-wired from many thousands of years of adaptation to make bad decisions. We are naturally driven, for example, to look at what other people are doing as a signal for what we should do.

When we lived as hunters and gatherers, this may have helped us survive by forcing us to pay attention to what was working for others to survive. The downfall is that we are naturally compelled to follow the crowd. We can't help it. We want to act like sheep, but are often led to slaughter by those who are shrewd enough to understand human nature.

If you learn anything from history class, learn this—people think they are smarter than they really are most of the time, are easily swayed by greed and fear, overestimate their skills, and assume wrongly that the future will be like the recent past. All of this is programmed into us because of centuries of survival as hunters and gatherers. Now that we live in modern times, however, the habits that create prosperity are different than they were a few hundred years ago.

Here is a short list of known, scientifically verified ways the human brain is designed to trick us:
1. **Representativeness** (aka fitting things into stereotyped categories)

   a. Example—researchers found that stock analysts overestimated the future performance of stocks that had done well recently and far underestimated the performance of stocks that had performed poorly.

2. **Overconfidence**

   a. Test—The Dow Jones Industrial Average (DJIA) closed in 1998 at 9,181. As a price index, the DJIA does not include reinvested dividends. If the DJIA were redefined to include all reinvested dividends since May 1896, when it commenced at a value of 40, what would the value have been in 1998? In addition to writing down your best guess, also write down a low guess and a high guess, so that you feel 90 percent confident the true answer lies between your high guess and your low guess.

   b. Answer—652,230

   c. Lesson: Humans get surprised by the market, because they don't set up wide enough expectations.

3. **Get-Even-itis** (loss aversion)

a. In 1995, Nicholas Leeson bankrupted a 232-year old bank, Barings PLC, when, while trying to cover up trading losses for his division, he incurred a single loss of $1.4 billion. Whoops!

b. Lesson: Humans have a tendency to avoid losses at all costs, which causes them to hold on to losing investments too long.

4. Confirmation Bias

a. Investors only look for confirming evidence and ignore disconfirming evidence. (Einhorn & Rogharth, 1978).

b. Example—Investors still use a sentiment index to time the market, even though studies have shown that the index has absolutely no correlation to stock market returns. Instead, investors who use it argue that the index has been right in the past, therefore it must be right in the future. They forget to look for evidence to prove themselves wrong.

c. Lesson: Humans look for evidence that they're right. They avoid evidence that shows they're wrong.

So, before you go trying to find a better way to invest your money, stop and consider your own psychology for a moment. The reason I suggest this simple, easy-to-follow strategy is because any other strategy I used introduces lots of emotional and psychological bias. We tend to make stupid decisions when we don't have a simple, automatic strategy. That's the whole point of the system.

If you don't do stupid stuff, you tend to get pretty good results.

It's that simple!

An Emotional Game
So, now that you're starting to understand the importance of psychology, let's talk about what kinds of emotions you're going to face during this wild ride to becoming wealthy!

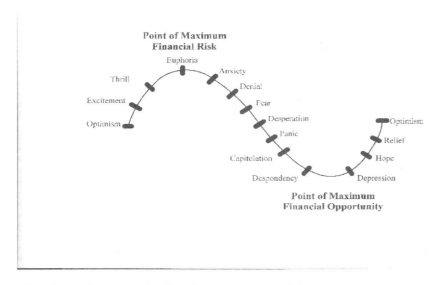

The chart above basically shows you two things:

1. When the market is overvalued, people tend to be "greedy," which means they pay more than what a security is worth, assuming the price will continue to go up. Think "Housing Bubble" or "Dot Com Boom of the 1990s."
2. When the market is undervalued, people tend to be "fearful." They sell when they should buy, assume the world will be bad forever, and avoid risk when the market actually has little risk.

During your life, you will see more than a few boom-bust cycles. Your job as an investor is to not let greed set in when the market seems to keep going up and up and up. Keep buying when the market is a real panic. Over the long run, your returns will kill the average investor's return, because you acted smarter when it counted.

Stick to a simple indexing strategy and buy regularly, being sure you don't let the news or the talking heads on TV trick you into deviating to the left or to the right. Stick to the course ahead and you'll win. That brings us to another point.

If the market crashes, don't worry. Be happy. A crash means you get to buy cheap stock. It's not the price now that counts, after all. It's the amount of money you have when you get to thinking about what you want to do with the rest of your life after work. It works in your favor for prices to be low, so that you can continue to buy cheap stock. Eventually, the market will correct and your good decisions will pay off.

Likewise, when the market goes up for a long time, be wary. All good things must come to an end. This is the exact opposite of how most people invest and why they fail. Most people, when they see others doing well in the stock market, try to get into the market. It's usually at that time when the market crashes and the "greedy" investor loses his money—inevitably selling at the bottom of the market because he's now become "fearful."

A Final Thought
It is almost inevitable that you will see a company one day (such as Facebook or Tesla) and assume that it's a great company and destined to grow to the sky. All your friends will be using it and, to you, it will be a no-brainer. You will be tempted to sell your index mutual fund and buy the new hot stock. This is completely normal. In fact, if you're making money with your simple strategy, you'll probably start to pay more attention to the stock market and develop some understanding for how things work.

Your hot stock pick might be right. In fact, it might be REALLY right and you might be able to make more money in the short term. But alas—most stock picks do about as well as your index—and, after fees and commissions, your performance actually suffers. I urge you to take note when you get the desire to change strategies. This is your caveman programming trying to trick you. Leave your money alone, and stick to your guns. You'll be glad you did. Indexing almost always works better over the long run. Now you're equipped to see when your psychology is trying to dupe you.

Chapter Seven

Why You Should NEVER EVER Touch Your

Investments

A Dramatic Warning

The goal of this chapter is to accomplish one thing—that no matter what comes your way—avalanches, snow blizzard, tornadoes, or even swarming herds of walkers; you will NEVER EVER withdraw any of your accumulated wealth until you are at least 65, no matter how much you think you need it.

This is such a critical discipline.

Most people will have an event in their lives that tempts them to pull money out of their savings account. It's just the way life works. Random events happen—some good and some bad. Most people don't believe, however, that the bad stuff will happen to them.

Unfortunately, it's just not possible for you to go through life without anything bad happening to you. The average person lives about 30,600 days. So, to put it one way, you have at least 30,600 chances for something bad to happen to you. Luckily, you also have the same number of chances for good things to happen.

You can expect to get into a tough spot at some point in your life. If you're mentally prepared, you'll get through it a lot easier.

Why bring this up?

I grew up in a middle-class family. I figured that life would continue being easy, and I'd wind up well off myself one day—no problem. My parents seemed to be successful, so why shouldn't I be? I had no worries. Success would surely find me.

The problem was . . . Early on in life I didn't have much drive or direction. I floated around for years, always wondering when I'd catch my break. Eventually, I found my way into a "big-boy job," working in an entry-level position for a large corporation. I worked there for years and saved little money, still wondering when my big break would happen.

After loyally working eight years for my employer, I started my own business. I was often told that starting a business was the best way to make it big. So I took my experience, plus the little money I had saved and applied it toward hiring others and creating a successful business. Unfortunately, not all businesses thrive, and I exited the business during the recent "Great Recession." I wasn't prepared for the economy to nearly collapse. Finding work, especially after owning my own business, was particularly hard for me. I scrambled to get work, but nothing came. Two months went by—then three—then six—and just like that, I was in a real pickle. I had to get cash somehow, and I started searching for it anywhere it could be found.

After all other areas of finding available funds were exhausted, in my desperation, I looked at the nest egg that was my 401k. All my net worth at the time was contained in that little savings account. But "I have to get some cash NOW!" I thought. So, I did what any normal human being in my position would do. I liquidated my 401k.

To this day, that is one of the stupidest decisions I've ever made. I'm still kicking myself about it. Most people don't understand why I think of that decision as one of my densest moments. They don't realize that the decision I was really making concerned short-term stability vs. long-term security.

Most people who live paycheck to paycheck don't understand the concept of long-term security. They've never had it, they don't know what it feels like, and they sure as heck don't know how to get it. They're clueless—sometimes because of the way they were raised and other times because they're not wired to think long-term.

In my situation, I was in so much pain and stress (because I had so little income) that I forced myself to take my eye off the ball—to stop focusing on long-term security.

Before things fell apart, I was building savings that would work for me. I was focused on building enough wealth that the interest my money generated would be enough to live on for the rest of my life. I'd never have to worry about working for a paycheck again. I could wake up when I wanted, have a nice breakfast, go play golf, and then take an afternoon nap; and no one would be able to tell me I couldn't. Long-term financial security gives you freedom and lets you write the rules. That's what I wanted. That's what I was working toward—until I liquidated the account.

When the account was cashed out, I traded that long-term security for short-term stability. I could pay my bills again. I didn't have to put only $10 of gas in the car at one time and shop at the discount grocery store. I had more time to find a job. All of those things gave me relief, but they didn't solve my real problem. And now, my personal wealth building was back at square one. I was financially starting over, but now I was 20 years older.

I had three girls to raise and bills to pay. The economy was not great, and at any time, business could begin to make cutbacks. I could always be back at square one, over and over again.

What I learned from that mistake was to always focus on building long-term financial security, even at the expense of short-term financial stability. Of course, sometimes it's just not possible, but if you can weather the storm, you come out stronger and much closer to your goals.

Here are more good reasons people take money out of their accounts and ruin their chances of retiring rich:

- They lose their job and need cash.
- To impress a future spouse with a nice ring, wedding, and/or honeymoon.
- To buy a new house.
- To pay for childcare related expenses.
- They have a medical emergency.
- To pay for a deceased loved-one's funeral.
- To pay off student loans.
- They become disabled and need income.

Here are some possible acceptable reasons to raid your accumulated wealth:

- To pay college tuition if you can't get loans.
- To fund a business.
- To pay off high-interest credit card bills.

To make my point clearer, it's necessary to understand just how much money you're losing by pulling money out of your account early. Let's take a look at a real example, and see just how much money we're talking about.

Rob and Brent were friends who both worked at their local grocery store making $100 a week after taxes. From their efforts, they both saved about $2,000 a year inside a Roth IRA from age 16 to age 22. In addition, both invested the money in a low cost index mutual fund. By age 22, Rob's and Brent's Roth IRAs had a value of $18,044 each. Not bad for 22 years old.

Like most people, the boys graduated college and started their careers. Because they weren't earning much, they stopped putting money in their Roth IRAs, but let the accounts continue to grow. Then a few years later, Rob got married, started looking at buying a house, and his wife got pregnant. Money got tight, and Rob decided to liquidate his Roth IRA.

At 30 years old, Rob's and Brent's account values were $35,954 each.

Brent got married too, but told his wife before they started dating seriously about his desire to not touch the money in his Roth IRA and to live within his means. She was onboard, and they managed their finances so that they didn't have to dip into their savings. Brent eventually started saving and investing money in his employers 401k plan, while letting his Roth IRA continue to grow. As a result, at age 65, Brent's Roth IRA account value was $733,959 and, along with his 401k savings, he was able to retire to a nice home by the beach in Florida, knowing he would never have to work another day in his life.

So, what's the lesson? Rob gave up almost $700,000, because he was chasing short-term stability instead of long-term security. He wasn't thinking about the long-term consequences of his decision. Big mistake.

Most people don't look at their wealth-building accounts from the perspective of what it could be. Brent realized that, although his savings account wasn't big now, it would be in due time. He had patience, stuck to his plan, and let his money work for him—taking advantage of the law of compounding returns.

What Brent did wasn't rocket science. In fact, it's ridiculously simple. It's so easy, in fact, that most people don't believe it will work. They're use to making money the hard way—through lots of toil and sweat—but that's not how you get really wealthy. You have to work smarter—not harder.

Realize that tiny hinges swing big doors. Little actions today can have a huge impact in the distant future. Use that to your advantage. Save smart, set it, and then forget it. Once you've put some money in savings, do your best to never touch it. One day you'll be glad you did.

So, that's it. You know where I stand on this issue. Never, under any circumstance, touch your Roth IRA. Guard it with your life and don't let anyone rob you of its gold. If you do this, it's almost guaranteed that you'll have tremendous financial options later in life.

Chapter Eight

The Roth IRA: Learn the Rules

Let's Pretend It's a Game

I like games. Before you can play a new game, you have to read the rules. The rules are clearly not the most exciting part of the game, but they are important. Without knowing the rules, there's no structure to the game. Opening a Roth IRA and knowing how a Roth works are important, because they give structure to how you start investing and creating wealth.

Here's the really good news about the rules, they're simple and, better yet, most of them aren't going to apply to you. For example, if you're old, you can contribute more, it's called a "catch-up" contribution, and it's not a condiment. You don't need to know about that. If you're married, a nonworking spouse can open an account and contribute, based on the working spouse's income.

Again, that's not going to apply here. I'm not going to suggest that later in life you won't want to learn some of the more advanced rules, but for now, you only need to learn the basics of how to get started, so I'm going to keep it simple.

The Rules—Teenager Edition
1. Age

This one is straightforward. There is no minimum age to open a Roth. If you are under the age of majority in your state (usually 18 years old), you'll need a parent or guardian to open the account with you. It will automatically become your account when you reach the age of majority.

2. Contributions

You're limited to a maximum annual contribution of $5,500 (as of 2014). What you contribute must be earned income. If you earn less than $5,500, you may only contribute up to the maximum amount earned. For example, if you have a summer job and earn $2,000, then you can only contribute a maximum of $2,000.

3. Income Limits

I'm going to mention this just because there's a small chance that it could apply if you're a little older and reading this book. As a single person, to qualify for the maximum contribution, you must earn less than $114,000 per year (as of 2014). If you make more money, the maximum contribution limit begins to decrease.

4. Withdrawals

There are rules for how to withdraw money from the Roth account. At any time, you may withdraw, without penalty, the money you contributed to the Roth. If you put in $5,000, and the account is now worth $10,000, then you can withdraw the original $5,000 without penalty. If you withdraw (before your turn 59½) any of the gains made in your account, you'll pay tax on the gains plus a 10 percent penalty. Ouch and double ouch. The government gives you a few ways to wreck your wealth-building experience. However, this book is about creating wealth. Withdrawing your money before about age 60 is destroying your future wealth. The Roth isn't a savings account, and it isn't a way to save for college or a house. Save for those things in a different account.

5. College

Sad but true, investing money in a Roth could be considered money that's available to pay for college. If you are planning on asking for financial aid for college, it might be considered as part of the calculations for how much you're eligible for.

6. Savers Tax Credit

If you meet the following four conditions, you are eligible to claim a tax credit for your Roth contributions. This is huge.

1. You are 18 or over.
2. You are not a full time student.
3. You are not claimed on another person's tax return.
4. You make, as a single person, less than $27,750.

If you can say "yes" to those four conditions, you're eligible for up to a $1,000 tax credit. That's cash money back in your pocket. To claim the full amount for the tax year, you'd have to contribute at least $2,000 into your Roth.

7. No Forced Withdrawals

One thing that makes the Roth a wealth-building powerhouse is that there is no maximum age where you're forced to make withdrawals. Why is this important? Allowing wealth to grow unfettered is the key to building generational wealth. Generational wealth is where you have so much money, you'll leave plenty behind for your children and their children.

If you go on to have a financially successful career and use other tools available to provide for a comfortable life, you may not ever need to withdraw the money in your Roth. Your children may inherit your Roth and allow the balance to continue to grow and make tax-free withdrawals. How cool is that!

In this chapter, I've highlighted some major points about the Roth plan. This isn't a complete listing of all the rules, but rather an abridged version that highlights what's important for the plan in this book. If you are curious about all the details of the Roth IRA, I recommend visiting www.rothira.com or www.irs.gov/Retirement-Plans/Roth-IRAs.

Chapter Nine

How Rich People Really Act

Did you know that the average millionaire in the United States drives a used car, lives in a middle-class neighborhood in an average-size house, maintains a monthly spending budget, and saves most of their income? They don't buy the latest iPhone model, and they rarely buy designer clothes. They don't wear fancy jewelry, and they don't take month-long vacations to private islands in the Caribbean. The media portrays an image that all millionaires drive Lamborghinis and Maseratis, wear Gucci shoes and Rolex watches, and live in 30,000-square foot mansions by the beach, but that's not even close to the truth. Most millionaires are—well—unassuming.

Most millionaires are normal people with normal jobs who simply know that, in order to get wealthy, they must earn more than they spend. The bigger the difference between what you bring in and what you spend, the more you save. And the more you save, the more you have to invest and the faster you accumulate wealth.

Money In - Money Out = Total Savings

It's this simple math equation that the average millionaire takes seriously and builds his or her lifestyle around. For example, millionaires know that a good, low-mileage used car is almost no different than a brand new car, but costs 20 percent to 30 percent less. They know that a 2,500-square foot home in a nice neighborhood (when well taken care of) makes them just as happy as having a 30,000-square foot compound on the edge of Beverly Hills. They know that a good $6 hamburger makes them just as satisfied as the $100 filet mignon with truffle sauce from the nicest steak house in town.

For the average millionaire, wealth is not something to tell people about. Millionaires don't spend money just because they have it. To the wealthy, money is simply a tool that helps them solve problems and spend more time doing the things that bring them happiness. It's not something to be celebrated or flaunted. Most important, they know that money doesn't make you happy. It's your friends, family, work, and life experiences that really give you happiness.

Above all, millionaires don't worry much what people think about them. The wealthy don't try to impress others with their riches just to feel bigger and more important. People who become millionaires are happy with what they have and are content following their plan. Sure, sometimes they'll splurge like the rest of us, but they don't make it a habit. They are committed to their plan, and the opinion of others doesn't come into consideration.

I have a good friend, Matt, and his dad, we'll call him Tom, who became a millionaire pretty early in life. Tom graduated from medical school at age 24 and started practicing medicine at a small urban hospital. Within a few years, he'd bought a practice with another doctor and was making more than $500,000 a year. Tom invested in stocks and real estate and saved as much as he could, always buying used cars, living in a modest-size house, and even going so far as to buy all his groceries and clothes from Sam's Club in bulk to save money.

Within just a few years, Tom's fortune had ballooned to $15 million, and he had a cash flow of more than $20,000 per month, just from his real estate holdings. Yet, even at this level of wealth, you could never tell that Tom was rich. When he wasn't at the office, he wore old t-shirts and worn-out jeans. He drove an older model Ford truck. His leather wallet was even old and beat up. In fact, on the weekends he'd spend his time working in his own yard to save money on landscaping bills. Needless to say, Tom could have bought a Porsche 911 when he made his first million, and he could have chosen to live in a much larger, more impressive house, but Tom wasn't saving all that money just to be able to show it off. He was doing it because that was the smart thing to do for himself and his family.

Do yourself a favor and commit to earning more than you spend, no matter what it takes. Commit to using money as a tool to give yourself an easier life, and don't do it to impress others. That will solve a lot of your problems and, when you do get rich, people will like you a lot more.

$$$

Chapter Ten

Other Strategies for Life-Long Success

Understand What You Can Dominate

Bill Gates is well-known for being one of the richest people on the planet, but most people don't think of him as one of the greatest computer programmers ever. The fact is, Bill Gates was a programmer first and businessman second.

Bill was a strange kid, always attracted to large encyclopedias and books on technology. He read voraciously as a child and spent most of his time alone studying. He grew up in Seattle, Washington, attending one of the top prep schools in the country, Lakeside School. His love of technology led him to programming as a hobby from the school's computer lab. Because of the school's location and connections, Gates spent most of his free time (from the age of 13 to the age of 19) hacking out code on some of the most sophisticated computers in the country. It's estimated that Gates spent more than 10,000 hours in those computer labs during that time, so by his second year at Harvard, he was one of the top programmers in the country. Realizing that software was the future of the computer industry and understanding his talent, leaving Harvard to start Microsoft was an easy decision for Gates. Success, in his mind, was fairly certain. He was right.

Gates's story illustrates two important principles. First, Gates made a career out of something that he could be the best in the world at—something he'd willingly do for free that he was naturally designed for. Second, he put in 10,000 hours of real practice. If you think about it—how could Gates have NOT been at least moderately successful when you mix all those factors—genetics, work ethic, and being born at the right time in history?

Get my point?

This is simply Darwin's survival of the fittest theory played out in real life. Darwin thought that the most "fit" species would survive and the "weak" would die because either they couldn't attract a mate or they'd somehow get killed. In a free economic system, the "fittest" business people tend to rise to the top and make the most money, while the "weak" tend to get pushed out.

For people trying to make a living, "fitness" can be defined as skill; and skill is a function of aptitude and training. The higher your aptitude and training, the greater your skill. The person with the greatest mix of aptitude and practice will become the most skilled— aka the fittest. So, if you want to ensure you get rich, you need to do two things:

1. First, find out what you're really good at, and
2. Second, put in the practice (research shows that it takes 10,000 hours of practice to become an expert in something, so your goal should be 10,000 hours).

If you follow this little formula, you'll be miles ahead of your competition. About 99 percent of people won't put in the work it takes to be great at anything. If you can find what you enjoy and can be great at, and then spend your life trying to get better at it, people will seek you out and pay you large amounts of money to do what it is you do. From actors, musicians, screenwriters, comedians, doctors, lawyers, basketball players, salespeople, to race car drivers—the people at the top get paid almost all of the money, and the people at the bottom struggle or aren't even allowed to do the job at all. So realize, it's a law of nature and it works—practicing diligently in your area of strength will make you valuable to others, and that's what makes you rich.

Networking
In my local business newspaper each year, a ranking is published of what's called the "20 In Their 20s." The newspaper goes out and finds young, most up-and-coming people in our area and showcases their accomplishments and story. I am amazed every time I read it, because I see the same pattern over and over. What's the pattern?

Did they go to the best school? Nope.

Did they volunteer a lot? Nope.

Did they work harder than everyone else? Nope.

The only thing they really have in common is that they became known to people who mattered. Lots of people, who didn't make the list, work hard, do lots of good in their community, and are extremely smart, but that's not what gets you opportunity.

Opportunity is created through the people who know you, and the only way you can get to know people is through networking. Make lots of friends of all shapes and sizes and develop a reputation with them for making things happen.

So how do you network? Throw parties. Join clubs. Join a team. Go to church. Volunteer. Run for student government. Make friends! Lots and lots of friends! And make sure they know what you do well!

You see, once you become great at something, and lots of people know you as "that person who's really good at X," opportunities will flow your way. People will start calling you to help them with their projects. That's when you become "in-demand," and you can really start getting paid—and it all snowballs from there.

Networking, by the way, is cheap. While you're in school, people will tell you to focus on your grades. "Don't go out so much with your friends." "Don't waste your time on all those things, because it's a waste of time." I'll bet you one thing. The people who say that, aren't rich. Your relationships are just as important as your grades. Here's why:

Your grades may be a signal to the world of how smart you are and what you're able to accomplish, but the world tends to learn about your grades, your accomplishments, and how great you are through other people. It's like kinetic and potential energy. Good grades may give you "potential energy," but relationships release that potential—they make it "kinetic." You can have all the potential in the world, but unless you use it, it's worthless. That's why networking is so important.

Love Learning
Did you know that 80 percent of families in the United States have

not bought a book this year? That may not seem like a scary statistic, but it is. People who love to learn tend to buy books regularly, often buying multiple books every month in order to expand their knowledge. So, what this statistic tells us is that Americans don't make continuous learning a habit. In fact, only maybe 20 percent really take learning seriously.

But, why is learning important?

The fact is, it's a big, big world out there, and knowledge is increasing at a faster rate than at any moment in all history. For example, there will be more information uploaded to YouTube today than all the information created from the beginning of history until the year AD 2001. That's a lot of info! This means that learners have a distinct advantage over the rest of the world.

Learners will pick up knowledge quickly and use it to get better, while nonlearners will fall behind at a faster pace than they ever have. The people at the top will create more wealth and, as a result, leave less for nonlearners. So, if you want to succeed in the new millennium, you have to learn to love learning.

That's a good thing, though. The world is run by learners—and rightfully so. They're smarter and usually harder working. In fact, Fortune 500 CEOs read on average four to five books per month vs. the average American who reads fewer than one book per year. So, do yourself a favor: Learn to love learning.

How? Read books that get you excited. If you like rock climbing or horseback riding, go learn about it. If you want to understand how guys' brains are wired differently from girls' brains, go learn about it. Follow what you love. Don't worry (at first) about reading what other people think you should read. Don't feel forced to read *War and Peace,* just because someone says it's a classic and a must read. Just blaze your own trail, and let yourself fall in love with it.

Over time, you'll start to become curious about more things. You'll start to read about new topics. Although you may hate science now, learning about kite surfing may spark an interest in aerodynamics and physics. You never know.

And if you think you don't have time to read, take up this trick that's worked for thousands—audio books! Instead of jammin' Miley Cyrus' "Wrecking Ball," listen to an audio book when you're driving—just don't let your friends catch you! With an iPod, you literally have no excuse not to be reading. You can be learning while standing in line at McDonalds or at the beach getting a suntan. No excuses!

Eventually you'll grow into a real learner, and that's when you'll join the ranks of those CEOs who read four to five books a month, voraciously devouring new knowledge in order to improve their game. At that point, you'll be so far ahead of the pack, you'll probably never have to worry about getting a high-paying job again. It'll be in the bag.

So, those are my three bonus strategies for you to retire rich.

- Practice what you can be great at,
- Network, and
- Love learning!

If you do those three things for the rest of your life and follow our simple savings plan, you won't be able to avoid getting rich.

Chapter Eleven

A Sample Plan

The Game of Life

Have you ever played the game called *Life*? At the beginning of the game, each player picks out a playing piece shaped like a car and puts a little stick figure (pink for girls and blue for boys) in the driver seat. Throughout the course of the game, your car moves around the board, and the spaces on the board try to simulate the highlights, or in some cases lowlights, of the average person's life. You get a career, get married, buy a house, possibly have kids, buy insurance, and you can even play the stock market. Plus, there's a wonderful assortment of random life events. The objective of the game is to accumulate money and end up at Millionaire Acres.

Here's a plan to get you to Millionaire Acres.

We talked earlier about part-time jobs in high school and getting "earned income." Let's start there. If you don't have a savings account, open one. Have automatic payroll deposit set up so your money goes directly to the bank. Now you will work, get paid, and the money will automatically show up in your savings account.

As soon as you get a paycheck, open a Roth. If you're under 18, you will need your parents' help, but get it done. At the end of the book, I have some suggestions for companies that have low or no fees, indexed funds, and require a low initial investment. Set up an automatic transfer from your savings account into your Roth. All of the steps I just listed are important for your future.

You can decide for yourself, but I'd suggest you have $100 per week go directly into the Roth. If you're paid biweekly, then the first $200 from each paycheck goes into the Roth. Through your last two years of high school, you'll be able to save and invest about $10,000. Remember, as of 2014 there's a $5,500 limit on how much you can save in a Roth. At the end of the year, you'll be close to the limit. If you can max it out, **go for it.**

Those first two years may be a little rough, it may seem like all work and no play, but you'll have $10,000 or more in a great wealth-building account. If you add no more money, with an annual return of 8 percent, you'll have close to $350,000 tax-free by age 65. So you are over a third of the way to Millionaire Acres, and you're just getting out of high school!

How about that? We haven't even started the game of *Life* yet, and you're over a third of the way to Millionaire Acres. Congratulations!

Getting back to the game for a minute, the first decision in the game is whether to move your car down the path to college or not. Regardless of which way you choose, maintaining a steady part-time or fulltime job with a weekly contribution to your Roth is critical. If you don't go to college, you get off to a faster start in the game, but your career options are limited. Either way, you can still make it to the promised land of Millionaire Acres.

I know that not everyone reading this book is going to college. Some will choose the military, a trade school, a fast-track career program, take time off from school and work, or start a nondegree career. Whatever you choose, let's look at how to get to Millionaire Acres.

Option 1—Career First
You've chosen to take the high school diploma and start working fulltime. If you have to move out of your parents' house, that makes things tougher. You may need one or more roommates to share expenses and allow yourself to continue contributing to your Roth. Talk to your parents about staying in their house for a few more years. If they understand that you are saving and investing money for a brighter future, I'm sure they'd be more understanding. You may have to help with some expenses, but the extra income from more hours at a job should cover that.

Let's assume you continue to work one or two minimum-wage jobs that average a total of 40 hours per week. At $7.65 per hour, you will gross $306 per week. The net will be around $250, after taxes. Again, this will be higher or lower depending on your city and state. Each week put $100 a week into the Roth and use the other $150 a week for whatever expenses you have. If your parents help you with expenses, then start saving for a car, a house, or a rainy day.

The ages of 18 to 22 are critical here. This is where you have to maintain the commitment. Keep up with the $100 per week contributions, and at the age of 22 you will have about $42,000 invested. Even if you never contribute another dime for the rest of your life to another savings or investment account, you've already planted a seed that has a good chance to grow into about $1 million tax-free dollars during your life.

Option 2—College
The option to go to college will be financially costly. If you are on your own for tuition and expenses, think about how you could continue to contribute to your Roth during those years. Perhaps you work and attend school part-time and stretch the time it takes you to get a degree. Or, you might attend a community college to save on expenses and graduate with an associate's degree and then finish at a major university. I know that a college degree means something extra on a resume. It can be a requirement for many higher paying jobs and career tracks, but planting the seed for a million tax-free dollars is also important.

Signposts along Life's Road
Here are some financial signposts along the way to let you know that you're on track. At some points in time, these numbers may be way off due to a downturn in stock prices, but using history as a guide, we see that market averages tend to move higher over long periods of time. Having said that, I'll also say, "Past performance is no guarantee of future success." It's something every financial person will tell you when offering you an investment opportunity. Nobody can predict what the future holds, but keeping to the historical averages for broad indexes, such as the S&P 500, here's what to generally expect.

If you finish saving for retirement at age 22, with about $41,000 in your Roth that is invested in a low-cost S&P 500 indexed mutual fund, you'll have the following amounts at these ages.

Age 25—$53,000
Age 30—$77,000

Age 35—$114,000
Age 40—$167,000
Age 45—$246,000
Age 50—$361,000
Age 55—$530,000
Age 60—$780,000
Age 65—$1,145,000

There you go. Because of the hard work and sacrifice that you made for only six years of your life, even at a minimum-wage job, you can become a millionaire.

Don't Stop Investing

This book shows how investing $100 a week, with a part time job starting at age 16, and for six years in a diversified index fund inside a Roth IRA could grow to more than $1 million income tax-free dollars, using average historical stock market returns. Six years is a fair amount of time, but what if your six years were during a period of time where the market kept going higher? The stock market fluctuates every day, every month, and every year, but long downturns and crashes may take years to recover from.

So I suggest you keep setting aside some money, even if it's only $10 a week, into your Roth. The technical term is "dollar cost averaging," but the results are that by using the same amount of money, you'll buy more stock when the prices are lower and less stock when the prices are higher.

The Time Machine: How Is Life Treating You at 55?

Why is your 55th birthday important? If you followed the plan while you were young and made those faithful deposits into your Roth, you never touched the money, and the market chugged along with average annual gains of 8 percent, you'll have around half a million dollars. Lots of life events will be in the rearview mirror, and you will have a good idea of whether or not you will be relying on the Roth money for retirement.

If your career went well, and you've made wise investments, you might not even need the money in your Roth to live a comfortable life. Or, you may choose to withdraw just the dividend income from your investment. Just remember, that you never have to take money out of your Roth. It can even be willed to your children. If you lived to be 90 and never touched the money in your account, it's possible that you could have more than $10,000,000 to pass on to your family—income tax free—all because you followed a simple plan.

If your life events or personal choices, good or bad, didn't allow you to invest and save more money (and that's not uncommon), then it's a good idea to diversify away from 100 percent in stocks as you get older, even though it's a diversified stock index. The last thing you want to have happen is that you get close to retirement and the stock market crashes.

The End
It is my sincere wish that because you've read this book, you'll follow a different financial road than the one I traveled. I hope that with a basic understanding of the financial principles I've presented and a willingness to put them into action, you will begin to accumulate wealth for you, your family, and your children's family.

All the best,
Bill Edgar

List of Resources

A Couple of Brokerages

- Schwab.com— You can open a Roth IRA with no initial balance if an electronic transfer of a minimum of $100 per month is set up. This is a top choice for those who wish to follow our dollar-cost averaging index strategy. Also, the Schwab S&P 500 Index Fund has a very low expense fee of 0.09%.
- Vanguard— The annual $20 fee is waived if you sign up for electronic statements. The Vanguard 500 Indexed Fund requires a minimum account balance of $3,000 and a recently reported expense ratio of 0.17%.
- Online brokers E-Trade, ScottTrade, and OptionsXpress also offer online setup of a Roth IRA with typically no fees.

Investment Advisors for Advanced Planning

- For those requiring advanced financial management and wealth planning, contact: Northstar Financial Companies; Conshohocken, Pennsylvania; Steve Gerard at 610-629-6100 from 9:00 a.m. to 5:00 p.m. Eastern time.
- For those requiring simple payroll-deduction Roth IRA solutions, contact:
  Retirement Plan Advisors; Little Rock, Arkansas; Matthew Duckworth at mduckworth@retirementplanadvisors.com, or 501-615-8492 from 9:00 a.m. to 6:00 p.m. Central time.

Great Books about Money

- *The Millionaire Next Door,* by Thomas J. Stanley

- *The Richest Man in Babylon,* by George S. Clason
- *The Only Investment Guide You'll Ever Need,* by Andrew Tobias
- *The Intelligent Investor, Revised Edition,* by Benjamin Graham
- *Berkshire Hathaway Letters to Shareholders, 1965–2013,* by Warren Buffett and Max Olson (annual compilation)

Great Books about Personal Development

- *What Color Is Your Parachute?* by Richard N. Bolles
- *Outliers: The Story of Success,* by Malcolm Gladwell
- *The 7 Habits of Highly Effective People,* by Stephen R. Covey
- *Strengths Finder 2.0,* by Tom Rath
- *Finding Flow: The Psychology of Engagement with Everyday Life,* by Mihaly Csikszentmihalyi

IRS Overview of IRAs—

http://www.irs.gov/Retirement-Plans/Individual-Retirement-Arrangements-(IRAs)-1

Career Websites

- http://personality-testing.info/tests/RIASEC.php
- http://career.missouri.edu/career-interest-game
- http://www.self-directed-search.com/Default.aspx

About the Author

 Bill Edgar is the author of The Minimum Wage Millionaire: How a Part Time After School Job Can Change Your Financial Life. He is passionate about helping youth understand how to become wealthy. He lives in Elburn, Illinois, with his three nearly teenage daughters (who will all be required to read his book).

To contact Bill Edgar by email: waedgar@yahoo.com

A List of Companies in the S&P 500

3M
Abbott Laboratories
AbbVie
Accenture plc
ACE Limited
Actavis plc
Adobe Systems Inc
ADT Corp
AES Corp
Aetna Inc
AFLAC Inc
Agilent Technologies Inc
AGL Resources Inc.
Air Products & Chemicals Inc.
Airgas Inc.
Akamai Technologies Inc.
Alcoa Inc
Alexion Pharmaceuticals
Allegheny Technologies Inc.
Allegion
Allergan Inc
Alliance Data Systems
Allstate Corp
Altera Corp
Altria Group Inc
Amazon.com Inc
Ameren Corp
American Electric Power
American Express Co
American International Group, Inc.
American Tower Corp A
Ameriprise Financial
AmerisourceBergen Corp
Ametek
Amgen Inc.
Amphenol Corp A

Anadarko Petroleum Corp
Analog Devices, Inc.
Aon plc
Apache Corporation
Apartment Investment & Mgmt
Apple Inc.
Applied Materials Inc.
Archer-Daniels-Midland Co
Assurant Inc.
AT&T Inc.
Autodesk Inc.
Automatic Data Processing
AutoNation Inc.
AutoZone Inc.
Avalon Bay Communities, Inc.
Avery Dennison Corp.
Avon Products
Baker Hughes Inc.
Ball Corp
Bard (C.R.) Inc.
Baxter International Inc.
BB&T Corporation
Beam Inc.
Becton Dickinson
Bed Bath & Beyond
Bemis Company
Berkshire Hathaway
Best Buy Co. Inc.
BIOGEN IDEC Inc.
BlackRock
Block H&R
Boeing Company
Borg Warner
Boston Properties
Boston Scientific
Bristol-Meyers Squibb
Broadcom Corporation
Brown-Forman Corporation
C. H. Robinson Worldwide

CA, Inc.
Cablevision Systems Corp.
Cabot Oil & Gas
Cameron International Corp.
Campbell Soup
Capital One Financial
Cardinal Health Inc.
Carefusion
Carmax Inc.
Carnival Corp.
Caterpillar Inc.
CBRE Group
CBS Corp.
Celgene Corp.
CenterPoint Energy
CenturyLink Inc.
Cerner
CF Industries Holdings Inc.
Charles Schwab
Chesapeake Energy
Chevron Corp.
Chipotle Mexican Grill
Chubb Corp.
CIGNA Corp.
Cincinnati Financial
Cintas Corporation
Cisco Systems
Citigroup Inc.
Citrix Systems
CME Group Inc.
CMS Energy
Coach Inc.
Coca-Cola Enterprises
Cognizant Technology Solutions
Colgate-Palmolive
Comcast Corp.
Comerica Inc.
Computer Sciences Corp.
ConAgra Foods Inc.

Conoco Phillips
CONSOL Energy Inc.
Consolidated Edison
Constellation Brands
Corning Inc.
Costco Co.
Covidien plc
Crown Castle International Corp.
CSX Corp.
Cummins Inc.
CVS Caremark Crop.
D.R. Horton
Danaher Corp.
Darden Restaurants
DaVita Inc.
Deere & Co.
Delphi Automotive
Delta Air Lines
Denbury Resources Inc.
Dentsply International
Devon Energy Corp.
Diamond Offshore Drilling
DirecTV
Discover Financial Services
Discovery Communications
Dollar General
Dollar Tree
Dominion Resources
Dover Corp.
Dow Chemical
Dr Pepper Snapple Group
DTE Energy Co.
Du Pont (E.I.)
Duke Energy
Dun & Bradstreet
Eastman Chemical
Eaton Corp.
Ebay Inc.
Ecolab Inc.

Edison Int'l
Edwards Lifesciences
Electronic Arts
EMC Corp.
Emerson Electric
Ensco plc
Entergy Corp.
EOG Resources
Epeditors Int'l
EQT Corporation
Equifax Inc.
Equity Residential
Essex Property Trust Inc.
Estee Lauder Cos.
E-Trade
Exelon Corp.
Expedia Inc.
Express Scripts
Exxon Mobil Corp.
F5 Networks
Facebook
Family Dollar Stores
Fastenal Co.
FedEx Corporation
Fidelity National Information Services
Fifth Third Bancorp
First Energy Corp.
First Solar Inc.
Fiserv Inc.
FLIR Systems
Flowserve Corporation
Fluor Corp.
FMC Technologies Inc.
Ford Motor
Forest Laboratories
Fossil, Inc.
Franklin Resources
Freeport-McMoran Cp & Gld
Frontier Communications

GameStop Corp.
Gannett Co.
Gap (The)
Garmin Ltd.
General Dynamics
General Electric
General Growth Properties, Inc.
General Mills
General Motors
Genuine Parts
Genworth Financial Inc.
Gilead Sciences
Goldman Sachs Group
Goodyear Tire & Rubber
Google Inc.
Google Inc. C Shares
Graham Holdings Company
Grainger (W.W.) Inc.
Halliburton Co.
Harley-Davidson
Harman Int'l Industries
Harris Corporation
Hartford Fianancial Svc. Gp.
Hasbro Inc.
HCP Inc.
Health Care REIT, Inc.
Helmerich & Payne
Hess Corporation
Hewlett-Packard
Home Depot
Honeywell Int'l Inc.
Hormel Foods Corp.
Hospira Inc.
Host Hotels & Resorts
Hudson City Bancorp
Humana Inc.
Huntington Bancshares
Illinois Tool Works
Ingersoll-Rand PLC

Integrys Energy Group Inc.
Intel Corp.
IntercontinentalExchange Inc.
International Business Machines
International Game Technology
International Paper
Interpublic Group
Intl Flavors & Fragrances
Intuit Inc.
Intuitive Surgical Inc.
Invesco Ltd.
Iron Mountain Incorporated
Jabil Circuit
Jacobs Engineering Group
Johnson & Johnson
Johnson Controls
Joy Global Inc.
JPMorgan Chase & Co.
Juniper Networks
Kansas City Southern
Kellogg Co.
Keurig Green Mountain
KeyCorp
Kimberly-Clark
Kimco Realty
Kinder Morgan
KLA-Tencor Corp.
Kohl's Corp.
Kraft Foods Group
Kroger Co.
L Brands Inc.
L-3 Communications Holdings
Laboratory Corp. of America Holdings
Lam Research
Legg Mason
Leggett & Platt
Lennar Corp.
Leucadia National Corp.
Lilly (Eli) & Co.

Lincoln National
Linear Technology Corp.
Lockheed Martin Corp.
Loews Corp.
Lorillard Inc.
Lowe's Cos.
LSI Corporation
LyondellBasell
M&T Bank Corp.
Macerich
Macy's Inc.
Marathon Oil Corp.
Marathon Petroleum
Marriott Int'l.
Marsh & McLennan
Masco Corp.
Mastercard Inc.
Mattel Inc.
McCormick & Co.
McDonald's Corp.
McGraw Hill Financial
McKesson Corp.
Mead Johnson
MeadWestvaco Corporation
Medtronic Inc.
Merck & Co.
MetLife Inc.
Michael Kors
Microchip Technology
Micron Technology
Microsoft Corp.
Mohawk Industries
Molson Coors Brewing Company
Mondelez International
Monsanto Co.
Monster Beverage
Moody's Corp.
Morgan Stanley
Motorola Solutions Inc.

Murphy Oil
Mylan Inc.
Nabors Industries Ltd.
NASDAQ OMX Group
National Oilwell Varco Inc.
Neilsen Holdings
NetApp
NetFlix Inc.
Newell Rubbermaid Co.
Newfield Exploration Co
Newmont Mining Corp.
News Corporation
NextEra Energy Resources
NIKE Inc.
NiSource Inc.
Noble Corp.
Noble Energy Inc.
Nordstrom
Norfolk Southern Corp.
Northeast Utilities
Northern Trust Corp.
Northrop Grumman Corp.
NRG Energy
Nucor Corp.
Nvidia Corporation
Occidental Petroleum
Omnicom Group
ONEOK
Oracle Corp.
O'Reilly Automotive
Owens-Illinois Inc.
P G & E Corp.
PACCAR Inc.
Pall Corp.
Parker-Hannifin
Patterson Companies
Paychex Inc.
Peabody Energy
Pentair Ltd.

People's United Bank
Pepco Holdings Inc.
PepsiCo Inc.
Perkin Elmer
Perrigo
PetSmart, Inc.
Pfizer Inc.
Phillip Morris International
Phillips 66
Pinnacle West Capital
Pioneer Natural Resources
Pitney-Bowes
Plum Creek Timber Co.
PNC Financial Services
Polo Ralph Lauren Corp.
PPG Industries
PPL Corp.
Praxair Inc.
Precision Castparts
Priceline.com Inc.
Principal Financial Group
Procter & Gamble
Progressive Corp.
Prologis
Prudential Financial
Public Serv. Enterprise Inc.
Public Storage
Pulte Homes Inc.
PVH Corp.
QEP Resources
QUALCOMM Inc.
Quanta Services Inc.
Quest Diagnostics
Range Resources Corp.
Raytheon Co.
Red Hat Inc.
Regeneron
Regions Financial Corp.
Republic Services Inc.

Reynolds American Inc.
Robert Half International
Rockwell Automation Inc.
Rockwell Collins
Roper Industries
Ross Stores
Rowan Cos.
Ryder System
Safeway Inc.
Salesforce.com
SanDisk Corporation
SCANA Corp
Schlumberger Ltd.
Scripps Networks Interactive Inc.
Seagate Technology
Sealed Air Corp.
Sempra Energy
Sherwin-Williams
Sigma-Aldrich
Simon Property Group Inc.
SLM Corporation
Smucker (J.M.)
Snap-On Inc.
Southern Co.
Southwest Airlines
Southwestern Energy
Spectra Energy Corp.
St. Jude Medical
Stanley Black & Decker
Staples Inc.
Starbucks Corp.
Starwood Hotels & Resorts
State Street Corp.
Stericycle Inc.
Stryker Corp.
SunTrust Banks
Symantec Corp.
Sysco Corp.
T. Rowe Price Group

Target Corp.
TE Connectivity Ltd.
TECO Energy
Tenet Healthcare Corp.
Teradata Corp.
Tesoro Petrolium Co.
Texas Instruments
Textron Inc.
The Bank of New York Mellon Corp.
The Clorox Company
The Coca Cola Company
The Hershey Company
The Mosaic Company
The Travelers Companies Inc.
The Walt Disney Company
Thermo Fisher Scientific
Tiffany & Co.
Time Warner Cable Inc.
Time Warner Inc.
TJX Companies Inc.
Torchmark Corp.
Total System Services
Tractor Supply Company
Transocean
TripAdvisor
Twenty-First Century Fox
Tyco International
Tyson Foods
U.S. Bancorp
Union Pacific
United Health Group Inc.
United Parcel Service
United States Steel Corp.
United Technologies
Unum Group
Urban Outfitters
V.F. Corp.
Valero Energy
Varian Medical Systems

Ventas Inc.
Verisign Inc.
Verizon Communications
Vertex Pharmaceuticals Inc.
Viacom Inc.
Visa Inc.
Vornado Realty Trust
Vulcan Materials
Walgreen Co.
Wal-Mart Stores
Waste Management Inc.
Waters Corporation
Wellpoint Inc.
Wells Fargo
Western Digital
Western Union Co.
Weyerhaeuser Corp.
Whirlpool Corp.
Whole Foods Market
Williams Cos.
Windstream Communications
Wisconsin Energy Corporation
Wyndham Worldwide
Wynn Resorts Ltd.
Xcel Energy Inc.
Xerox Corp.
Xilinx Inc.
XL Capital
Xylem Inc.
Yahoo Inc.
Yum! Brands Inc.
Zimmer Holdings
Zions Bancorp
Zoetis

16663977R00046

Made in the USA
Middletown, DE
19 December 2014